How to Train Your Miniature Schnauzer

An Expert Guide to Smart Socialization Strategies for Caring, Grooming, and Raising a Confident Small Breed Dog

Finnley Crestwood

Copyright © 2024, Finnley Crestwood

Disclaimer

The information in this book is intended for general guidance on training. It is not a substitute for professional advice. Always consult with a veterinarian or certified dog trainer for tailored recommendations. The author and publisher disclaim any liability for actions taken based on the content of this book.

How to Train your
Miniature Schnauzer

Contents

Introduction

I'll never forget the first time I laid eyes on my Miniature Schnauzer puppy, Otto. As an experienced dog owner and trainer, I knew bringing home this lively, intelligent breed would be an adventure! Miniature Schnauzers are packed with personality and work ethic in a tiny wire-haired frame about 12-14 inches tall. Originally bred to be effective ratters on farms over a century ago, they're tenacious individuals who excel at agility, obedience, and tricks with correct motivation and training.

When 8-week-old Otto leaped out of his box at the breeder's, he locked eyes with me quickly with his distinctive Mini Schnauzer beard and bushy brows. I could already see his puppy wheels moving, evaluating how to keep me on my toes. True to pattern, within his first week home, teenage Otto had already learned to pop open cabinet latches with his nimble paws to ransack the treat bag. His ratter roots make hide-and-seek his favorite game, sniffing out ingeniously concealed toys in minutes.

Like many Miniature Schnauzers, Otto was clever as a whip. House training was no match for his tenacious attitude, learning the bells on the door to signify potty breaks within days. Commands like "sit", "paw", and "go find your bone" clicked quickly with treat motivation. His stuffed Kong toy kept him happily occupied for hours, gratifying his drive for activity.

But Otto wasn't all labor - Miniature Schnauzers thrive on being close to their people. He followed me from room to room, constantly wanting to be part of the action. A true velcro dog, he honed his "sit pretty" technique simply to win my attention for caressing and praise. His zeal charmed everyone he met, dog and human alike, with his hilarious whiskers twitching over his bearded smile.

Like many Miniature Schnauzers, Otto did have a stubborn streak. His training met teenage regression about 7 months when he concluded rules appeared optional. His innate barking tendency kicked in full force to demand walks, supper, and ball play on his schedule. With patience and consistency, we worked through the adolescent pranks. Regular exercise and training sessions became our unique bonding time, exhausting his brain and body.

Now at age 3, Otto remains my cherry, affectionate shadow, game for any adventure. My experiences teaching him extensively tested but ultimately rewarded my skills as a Mini Schnauzer owner. This breed keeps you fully involved with their sharp wit and athleticism! I'm so happy about the canine friend and tricks champ Otto has become through positive, patient training tailored to his breed's particular features.

The things I learned along Otto's training path taught me so much about Miniature Schnauzers. Despite their diminutive stature, they have big personalities and cravings for cerebral stimulation. Now I want to share my proven insider tips with you in this guide. If you're considering adding one of these energetic dogs to your home, you're in for an amusing trip. Miniature Schnauzers' intelligence permits so many possibilities - yet their independent nature means they thrive with a steady hand controlling their powers.

Let's go into the keys for efficiently training these gratifying "little big dogs" at every age and stage. With consistency, incentive, and playfulness, you'll establish an unbreakable friendship with your Miniature Schnauzer built on understanding and respect. So get ready...life with a Mini Schnauzer is anything but dull!

Chapter One

Understanding the Miniature Schnauzer

The History and Origins of the Breed

The Miniature Schnauzer is a small terrier breed that developed in Germany in the mid-to-late 19th century. They were formed from crosses between the Standard Schnauzer and lesser breeds like the Affenpinscher and Poodle. The idea was to create a smaller version of the Standard Schnauzer that could be an efficient ratter on farms, but also a companionable home dog.

The earliest definitive proof of the Miniature Schnauzer's development comes from portraits and texts in Bavaria in the 1860s and 1870s. In 1895, the first breed club for Miniature Schnauzers was created in Germany. The breed was previously called the Zwergschnauzer which means "dwarf schnauzer" in German. The moniker distinguishes them from their larger Standard Schnauzer counterparts.

Miniature Schnauzers quickly acquired popularity outside farms due to their alert, active demeanor, and robust health. City inhabitants praised their vermin-hunting skills and used them as watchdogs. Their unusual bearded cheeks and dense salt-and-pepper coats added to their visual appeal. Throughout the late 1800s and early 1900s, Miniature Schnauzers were bred specifically for their refined appearance, small size, and working qualities.

The original breed standard stipulated that Miniature Schnauzers should weigh 13 to 20 pounds and stand 12 to 14 inches tall. Over time, some breeding operations created even smaller lines, down to a tiny 5 pounds. But most breeders retained the original intended medium-small size.

Miniature Schnauzers were initially imported to North America around 1925. The American Kennel Club recognized them as a unique breed in 1926. Their popularity in the U.S. expanded substantially after World War II. Soldiers had encountered the dogs overseas and brought them home. Today they rank as one of the most popular breeds, beloved for being vigilant guard dogs yet of convenient tiny height.

Through single-minded breeding for their specific qualities over 100+ years, Miniature Schnauzers have developed an incredibly homogeneous breed. They are powerful, squarely formed dogs recognized anywhere by their rugged beards, arching bushy eyebrows, and harsh wiry coats. Their beginnings as a versatile ratter, farm dog, and pet friend are mirrored in their personality: vivacious, affectionate, and game for anything.

Miniature Schnauzer Characteristics and Temperament

The Miniature Schnauzer is regarded as being an enthusiastic, clever companion dog with plenty of personality. Here is an outline of the breed's essential traits and temperament:

Size and Appearance

- Height ranges from 12-14 inches tall at the shoulder - Weighs 11-20 pounds
- Rectangular, strong, and robust structure
- Long, thick, wiry outer coat with soft underneath
- Signature beard, bushy eyebrows, and mustache
- Coat comes in salt-and-pepper, black, or black-and-silver

Temperament

- Lively, alert, energetic dogs - Devoted and affectionate with families - May be reserved with strangers - Intelligent and trainable, but some can be stubborn - Territorial watchdogs who will bark at noises
- Playful and fun-loving throughout life - Good with children if socialized early - Can live in apartments but need daily exercise

Activity Level

- Require 30-60 minutes of exercise daily - Enjoy vigorous walks, running, and trekking - Eager to play games like fetch and tug-of-war
- Make good jogging or running companions - Their ratter heritage makes them diggers - Prone to pursuing small animals if not trained

Grooming Needs

- Require frequent brushing and combing - Unique salt-and-pepper coats need hand stripping - Removing dead hairs helps preserve texture
- Beards need regular washing and combing - Nails should be clipped regularly

Training Tips

- Respond very well to positive reinforcement - Food rewards are fantastic motivation for training - Early socialization is crucial to minimize wariness - May be predisposed to dominate behaviors without guidance - Bored Schnauzers can turn destructive - Need a firm but patient hand - not harsh methods

Overall, the Miniature Schnauzer is great for individuals seeking a tiny, strong dog with adequate energy for play and exercise. Their attentiveness makes them good guard dogs, but they also bond strongly with their people. With training and socialization from puppyhood, they may thrive in any setting as vibrant, loving companions.

Health Considerations for the Miniature Schnauzer

In general, Miniature Schnauzers are a solid, healthy breed thanks to decades of careful breeding. However, like all dogs, they are prone to various health issues that owners should be aware of. Here is a summary of the most prevalent health conditions facing Miniature Schnauzers:

Hereditary Eye Diseases

Miniature Schnauzers can develop many inherited eye disorders including:

- Cataracts - cloudiness in the lens causing blurred vision - Glaucoma - increased eye pressure affecting the optic nerve
- Progressive retinal atrophy - progressive vision loss owing to retina degradation

Reputable breeders test breeding dogs for these illnesses to lessen risk. Owners should also have their Schnauzer's eyes tested annually by a vet.

Hyperlipidemia

This disorder produces elevated triglyceride levels in the blood. It can lead to episodes of pancreatitis. Signs include vomiting, loss of appetite, and stomach pain. It is controlled by a low-fat diet and medicines.

Bladder Stones

Miniature Schnauzers are prone to both calcium oxalate and struvite bladder stones. These stones irritate the bladder lining and can cause blood in the urine, frequent urination, and trouble peeing. Special nutrition and sometimes surgery are required for treatment.

Liver Disease

A hereditary mutation predisposes Miniature Schnauzers to persistent active hepatitis leading to liver failure. Signs include lack of appetite, vomiting, jaundice, and ascites. Lifelong medication and diet adjustment can help manage it.

Diabetes Mellitus

An inability to regulate blood sugar levels commonly develops in the breed, necessitating daily insulin injections and strict monitoring of blood glucose. Signs include increased thirst, increased urination, and weight loss.

Allergies

Both food and environmental allergies are fairly common in Miniature Schnauzers. Symptoms including itchy skin, ear infections, and hot areas can develop. Diagnosis via exclusion diets and therapies such as antihistamines, immunotherapy, or steroids may be needed.

Joint Problems

Some Miniature Schnauzers will have hip and elbow dysplasia as well as luxating patellas (dislocated kneecaps). Limping, difficulty getting up, and loss of muscle mass may be noted. Weight management and joint supplements can help.

Heart Disease

Middle to older Schnauzers might have mitral valve disease causing the heart to expand. Coughing, difficulty breathing, and intolerance to exercise may occur. Various drugs are used to control symptoms.

Cancer

Miniature Schnauzers have greater incidences of various cancers such as mammary tumors, melanoma, and pancreatitis. Routine vet checkups and early care for any lumps or bumps are suggested. Early detection and treatment give the greatest odds.

In summary, Miniature Schnauzers are prone to a number of genetic health problems. Choosing a puppy from health-tested parents can help avoid dangers. Owners should cooperate closely with their vet for prompt preventative and wellness care. With diligent supervision and quality nutrition and lifestyle, most Miniature Schnauzers can live happy and healthy lives for 12-14 years or longer.

Chapter Two

Preparing for Your Miniature Schnauzer Puppy

Puppy Proofing Your Home

Preparing your home for a Miniature Schnauzer puppy will take some puppy-proofing, but it's well worth the effort to keep your pup safe. Here are some pointers on how to efficiently puppy-proof your home:

Block Access to Cables and Hazards

Puppies love to chew, and cables and cords can be an attractive nuisance. Tape down or hide any unsecured cords for computers, phones, and other equipment. Place plastic cord covers over any exposed electrical cords. Use furniture to prevent access to entertainment systems. Remove dangling pull cords from blinds and curtains.

Scan at Puppy Height

Get down on your hands and knees to view your home from a puppy's perspective. Look for any little objects they could swallow such as pins, buttons, screws, or toy pieces. Make sure you pick up medications, home cleaners, and dangerous things that puppies could consume from low shelves or bathroom cabinets.

Secure Trash Cans

Trash has many exciting aromas and flavors for puppies, which can lead to messy raids if cans are accessible. Use child locks or latches to secure lids shut. Place cans in cupboards or closets if feasible. Never leave garbage bags out unattended.

Use Baby Gates

Install adjustable baby gates to block off places like kitchens, staircases, and utility rooms that you don't want your puppy walking into unsupervised. Make sure gates are tall enough so your Schnauzer won't jump over them once they are grown. Pressure mount gates are easy for human passage.

Protect Valuables

Keep collectibles, heirlooms, and expensive furniture secured in glass display cases or blocked by durable pet gates. Restrict access if needed until the puppy has passed the gnawing stage. Provide plenty of acceptable chew toys to divert attention from antiques and heirlooms.

Secure Houseplants and Wires

Puppies may be enticed to play with or chew on household plants. Move hazardous plants fully out of reach or use harsh anti-chew spray. Place live wires to devices within a protective enclosure. Tie up excess electrical cords neatly.

Invest in Pet-Safe Cleaning

Replace any harsh chemical cleansers with enzyme-based pet-safe cleaners. Puppies are likely to lick surfaces. Vinegar, hydrogen peroxide, and dish soap are good pet-safe disinfectants. Keep all cleaning products protected in cabinets.

Protect Floors and Walls

Cover wood, laminate, and tile floors with cushioned runner rugs to avoid slips. Stain-resistant tie-up rugs under water bowls help contain messes. Install wall corner guards to avoid wall chewing damage in puppy zones.

Prepare a Puppy Play Area

Designate a safe, confined play space like a playpen, puppy room, or gated area to keep your puppy when you are busy or gone. Stock it with toys, a crate fitted with bedding, scratch pads, and freshwater. Rotating toys will retain their interest.

Start Training Right Away

Begin training your puppy right immediately on what rooms/areas are off-bounds. Use a forceful "No" with redirection when they venture to banned zones. Praise and reward them for remaining in designated puppy zones. Be patient - it will take time for them to understand family norms.

Puppy proofing takes some time and work upfront, but prevents costly damage long-term. Prepare issue zones based on your puppy's particular qualities. Schnauzers are bright and investigative dogs, so being proactive about safety and boundaries from day one is a must.

Shopping List for Supplies

Preparing your home for a new Miniature Schnauzer entails stocking up on all the important things they will need. Use this thorough shopping list to get fully equipped before your puppy arrives:

For Feeding

- High-quality dry puppy kibble
- Shallow dish for food
- Slow feed bowl to prevent scarfing
- Water bowl(s) for separate rooms
- Interactive food toys like Kong

For Sleeping

- Sturdy crate with divider panel
- Washable crate pads and bedding
- Designated puppy sleeping areas

For Containment and Safety

- Tall adjustable pet fences for rooms
- Exercise pen or puppy pen
- Baby locks for cupboards
- Pet barrier for electronics
- Power cord protectors
- Puppy housetraining pads

For Training

- Clicker for marking behaviors
- Variety of soft training treats
- Treat pouch for hands-free use
- Enzyme cleaner for accidents
- Positive training guidebook

For Identification

- Collar with ID tag
- Microchip identification
- GPS dog tracker (optional)

For Grooming

- Bristle brush for coat
- Metal comb for dematting
- Slicker brush for finer areas
- Nail clippers and file
- Ear cleanser
- Dog shampoo and conditioner
- Dog toothbrush and toothpaste

For Exercise and Play

- Variety of chew toys
- Interactive food toys
- Fetch balls and flying discs
- Tug rope and squeaker toys
- Teething toys
- Puzzle toys for cerebral stimulation

For Travel

- Comfy dog crate

- Seatbelt harness or restraint

- Water bottles and collapsible bowls

- Waste bags, paper towels, wipes

- First aid kit for dogs

For Grooming

- Rubber-tipped grooming forceps

- Stripping knife for coat care

- Non-slip bath mat

- Towels

For Health

- Basic first aid supplies

- Digital thermometer

- Tick/flea prevention and treatment

- Fish oil supplements

- Cleaning wipes and hand sanitizer

Shopping early ensures you have everything you need for your pup's first days in their new home. Introduce supplies gradually to make the changeover pleasant and comfortable. With the necessities in place, you'll both be set up for success!

Finding a Reputable Breeder or Rescue

Finding your Miniature Schnauzer from a trustworthy source is crucial to receiving a happy, healthy puppy. Take time studying breeders or rescues to discover the best fit.

Working With a Reputable Breeder

- Locate breeders via referrals, AKC marketplace, and shows.

- Confirm health testing on sire and dam. Key tests: eyes, bladder, liver, knees.
- Ask about past puppy health and longevity.
- Ensure the breeder vets prospective purchasers.
- Choose a stable temperament, oversize or color.
- Expect to sign a contract, and pay a deposit of roughly $500.
- Be ready to wait – good litters have waiting lists.

Questions to Ask

- How often do you breed dogs? Litters per year?
- Do you show any of your dogs in conformation or events?
- What health and temperament certificates do the sire and dam have?
- How have you socialized and stimulated the puppies thus far?
- What is the health guarantee?
- Will you take a puppy back at any stage if needed?

Red Flags

- Producing too many litters every year per dog.
- Willing to transport puppies under 8 weeks old.
- No health testing or promises on parents.
- Unable or unwilling to show parents on premises.
- Pressuring purchasers, first come first served.
- No interview screening of purchasers.

Working With Rescues and Shelters

- Research nonprofit Miniature Schnauzer rescues locally and nationwide.
- Fill out a written application with lifestyle facts, references, and commitments.
- Understand adoption policies, contracts, and fees before picking a dog.
- Ask about medical history and any behavior difficulties.
- Expect obligatory vet visits immediately after adoption.
- Be ready to change expectations on age, fitness, and training.

Adoption Process

- Complete the interview and home check if possible.
- Sign adoption contract and pay money, frequently $300 - $500.
- Receive the adoption packet with all vet records.
- Potentially set up a trial period at home.
- Receive behavioral and training help.
- Give the dog time to settle - months even!

Key Benefits

- Give an adult Schnauzer a second chance.
- Avoid puppy stages - the dog's personality is obvious.
- Learn all background medical and behavioral details.
- Often less costly than purchasing from a breeder.
- Gain satisfaction in rehoming a dog in need!

In general, trustworthy sources should thoroughly vet you as the prospective owner as much as you vet them. Finding a happy, healthy Miniature Schnauzer may involve serious search effort and patience. But the final result will be years of friendship with your ideal canine partner!

Chapter Three

Bringing Home Your Puppy

Preparing for the First Day and Night

The first day and night home with your Miniature Schnauzer puppy is a wonderful milestone! With some preparation, you can help your puppy feel comfortable and set them up for success. Here are some tips:

Puppy-Proof and Set-Up Areas

- Thoroughly puppy-proof your home and yard. Block access to hazards and valuables.
- Designate a major play/living area with food, bed, toys, and pads.

- Set up an enclosed sleeping place or open crate.
- Attach ID tags to their collar. Consider a microchip as a backup.
- Keep early play sessions brief to minimize overstimulation.

Choose an Optimal Arrival Time

- Aim for late morning or early afternoon arrival time.
- Allows you to settle the puppy before an evening ritual.
- Gives you daylight hours to interact, play, and start bonding.

Prepare a Potty Zone

- Pick an outside toilet area and take the puppy to it often.
- Initially go out every 30-60 minutes for toilet breaks.

- Use a leash to direct them; praise and reward successes.
- Consider an indoor solution like pads if you live in an apartment.

Introduce Your Home Slowly

- Limit first-day access to one or two puppy-proofed rooms.
- Gradually add household areas over consecutive days.
- Make introductions positive with delectable food and compliments.
- Pay close attention and redirect any unpleasant conduct sternly.

Keeping things low-key and focused on addressing basic requirements prevents overstimulation. Take it slow and allow your puppy to lead the way in what they are ready for in their new home.

Prepare for the First Night

- Simulate the litter environment with plush animals or a heartbeat pillow.
- Place the crate or enclosed bed in your bedroom for proximity.
- Offer numerous chew toys to help divert from being apart from littermates.
- Expect some fussing - respond minimally to encourage self-soothing.

Accidents and Clean-Ups

- Expect mistakes and tidy them up without scolding. Just redirect firmly outdoors.
- Limit liquids 2-3 hours before bedtime to prevent nighttime bathroom demands.
- Set an alarm to take the puppy out at least once overnight. Praise potty success.
- Thoroughly clean all accidents with an enzymatic cleanser to remove odors.

With planning, patience, and preventative precautions, your first 24 hours with your Mini Schnauzer pup will go smoothly. These stages set you both up for bonding and help your puppy feel comfortable and secure.

House Training

House training a Miniature Schnauzer puppy takes effort, consistency, and diligent supervision. Here is an overview of effective techniques:

Establish a Routine

Take your puppy out first thing in the morning, after naps, playtime, meals, and every 30 minutes to an hour in between. Frequent toilet breaks are necessary, especially for young dogs. Dogs learn best with predictability.

Choose a Bathroom Spot

Pick a specific outside potty place and always walk your puppy there on a leash. Provide lots of praise and incentives when they go in the correct spot. The fragrance reminds them to go. Loose leash management is needed to prevent wandering to the wrong spot.

Watch for Signals

Recognizing toilet cues like circling, sniffing, squatting, or growing silent allows you to swiftly scoop up your puppy and move them to the right restroom zone before they have an accident. Supervise closely while house training.

Use a Crate

When you can't immediately supervise, keep your puppy confined in their crate. Most won't soil a sleeping place. Space stays tiny employing a divider so they won't eliminate in one end. Never use the container for punishment though.

Reward and Praise

Celebrate successful outdoor toilets with over-the-top praise, pets, treats, and joy. This positive reinforcement is the best strategy to drive excellent elimination practices. Clean up any accidents carefully without criticizing.

Be Patient

House training takes months of consistency, not days. There will be mishaps along the road. Stick to a regular schedule, don't provide too much freedom too quickly, and keep at it. Your puppy's bladder control matures with time.

Troubleshooting Setbacks

If you encounter a frustrating plateau, go back to basics. Limit freedom, strengthen oversight, and reward success. See your vet to rule out a medical condition. Thoroughly clean all indoor mishaps to remove fragrance triggers.

Some Miniature Schnauzer pups may take longer to be entirely house-trained, up to a year even. But following these recommendations regularly from day one means you are putting your puppy up for eventual success.

Socializing Your Puppy

Early socialization is vital for Miniature Schnauzers to grow into confident, sociable friends. It should start as soon as you bring your puppy home. Here are tips:

Expose to New Surfaces

Get your puppy walking on diverse surfaces such as tile, linoleum, carpeting, gravel, grass, dirt, and puddles. Have them climb ramps and steps. Introducing fresh ground textures develops confidence.

Meet New Dogs

Arrange for calm, vaccinated adult dogs to meet your puppy one-on-one. Let them socialize on walks or in gated areas under your supervision to acquire excellent manners and communication. Avoid dog parks until completely immunized.

Introduce People

Invite friends and neighbors over regularly. Include people of all ages, appearances, and abilities. Give them sweets to develop pleasant associations. Teach youngsters proper interactions.

Experience Noises

Play recordings of sounds like fireworks, thunderstorms, sirens, or shouting at low volumes. Pair with treats to counter sensitivity to loud noises. Exposing your pet to variety minimizes over-reaction.

Explore Objects

Allow your dog to investigate new items like umbrellas, balloons, bins, bikes, or appliances in your home or yard. Show them these are not terrifying when introduced appropriately. Rotate toys to preserve novelty.

Take on Car Rides

Take your puppy on frequent short car journeys to positive destinations like a drive-thru or park. Make travel fun from the start and they will grow into good riding buddies. Use a locked container or harness.

Train Handling

Handle paws, ears, muzzle, teeth, and body often from early on. Check nails and brush fur. Getting acclimated to human contact prevents subsequent sensitivity. Always stay positive.

Socialize Daily

Aim for numerous fresh exposures each day in the first few months in safe, controlled settings. Go at your pup's pace and keep experiences upbeat. Proper socialization prevents complications down the way.

The more sights, noises, surfaces, smells, animals, and people your Mini Schnauzer encounters in a favorable environment early on, the more comfortable and confident they will be as an adult dog. Make interaction a priority starting the first day home.

Chapter Four

Basic Training Techniques

Clicker Training

Clicker training is a positive, reward-based strategy that works incredibly well for Miniature Schnauzers. Here's an introduction to effectively utilizing a clicker:

Choose a Clicker

- Use a plastic box-style clicker that generates a steady loud "click" sound.
- The piercing sound denotes the exact periods of desired activity.
- Keep the clicker in a pocket or purse for quick access.

Charge the Clicker

- To associate click with reward, click then immediately treat 10-20 times before training.
- This charges the clicker as a secondary reinforcer. The click conveys "treat coming!"

Time Precisely

- Click the instant your puppy does what you want - not after.
- Timing is critical: click while the action is occurring or just completed.
- Click only once for each prize to keep its significance.

Give Reward

- Quickly follow each click with a delectable food reward.
- Vary snacks - little portions of genuine meat, cheese, and chicken work nicely.

- Alternate reward with pets and praise sometimes too.

Use Sparingly

- Only click desired behaviors, not just any activity. Be precise.
- Avoid over-clicking and only award the best tries at a skill.
- This retains the significance and intensity of the click.

Add a Cue

- Once a behavior is learned via clicker, assign a verbal or hand cue before the action.
- Say "Sit" right before clicking a seat. Repeat until the dog expects and sits on cue.
- Cue first, behavior, click, reward.

Avoid Common Mistakes

- Don't wait too long to click after the activity occurs. Timing is essential.
- Don't encourage slow replies or inappropriate behaviors. Be precise.
- Don't rely simply on the clicker. Use praise too.
- Don't assign verbal cues too soon. Behavior must be learned first.

Troubleshooting

- If the dog loses interest, take a break or recharge the clicker with easy repetitions.
- Ensure you're clicking just once for each prize.
- Make sure food rewards are appealing and varied.

With regular brief sessions, Miniature Schnauzers react very well to clicker training. The sharp sound keeps children interested while the fast positive reinforcement shapes habits rapidly. Clicker training is entertaining, effective, and humane for both dogs and people.

Reward-Based Training

Reward-based training provides positive reinforcement to urge dogs to repeat desired behaviors. This force-free approach is particularly beneficial for Miniature Schnauzers. Here's how it works:

Identify Motivators

- Determine rewards for your specific dog values - food, toys, praise.
- Have a selection of tiny goodies accessible for training sessions. Real flesh works wonderfully.
- Always train when the puppy is attentive and eager to work for rewards.

Reward Desired Behavior

- As soon as your pup offers the action or behavior you want, mark it with a "Yes!" or click and give the reward.
- Be accurate and consistent. The award must be matched to the exact conduct.
- Gradually shape increasingly complicated skills by rewarding succeeding steps.

Use Variable Reinforcement

- Vary how often you reward consecutive successes: frequent at first, then less often.
- Reward intermittently to maintain the habit. Dogs work harder this way.
- For recognized talents, employ a variable ratio like awarding every 3rd or 5th repeat.

Employ Life Rewards

- Incorporate genuine rewards into training like throwing a ball, unlocking a door, and releasing to play.

- These are reinforcing because they give access to things your dog instinctively wants.

Avoid Punishment

- Never punish fear-based behaviors like shyness or submissive urination. This typically makes them worse.
- Harsh corrections can disrupt the human-animal relationship and hinder learning.
- If you need to stop an undesired activity, interrupt it neutrally, then redirect to what you want.

Troubleshoot Slow Progress

- Ensure the incentive is something your dog finds motivating.
- Break the skill into tiny progressive steps if needed.
- Rule out medical conditions inhibiting advancement through vet checkups.

- Consider sessions too long - finish at peak interest.
- Avoid repeating sessions to reduce boredom.

Patience is crucial! Persistently rewarding approximations and tiny achievements are how dogs learn. Miniature Schnauzers thrive on positive reinforcement strategies that inspire them to readily repeat behaviors. Reward-based training builds an outstanding partnership built on trust.

Understanding Dog Body Language

Learning to analyze your Miniature Schnauzer's body language is vital for recognizing their emotional condition and communication cues. Here's what to look for:

Face
- Relaxed eyes and mouth = content

- Tense eyes, lips drawn back = alert or aggressive

- Squinting eyes, avoiding look = scared

- Yawning = stress

Ears

- Erect, forward = alert, attentive

- Relaxed, natural position = neutral

- Flattened back = scared or submissive

- Perked back = confident, dominant

Tail

- Loose, natural = relaxed

- Slow wag = cautiously happy

- Fast wag = energetic, eager

- Tucked under = scared, uneasy

- Stiff, vibrating = alert, excited

Body

- Loose, wiggly = cheerful

- Crouched, lowered = insecure

- Piloerection (raised hair) = frightened

- Play bow = ready to play!

- Body block = lack of confidence

Mouth

-Open, tongue out = heated or stressed

- Panting heavily = anxiousness

- Louder noises like growls or barks express strong emotions

- Snarling or snapping = aggression

Vocalizations

- Short barks = alert or greetings

- Repetitive barks = needs, alarms, boredom

- Long howls = wanting comfort or attention

- Growls = warning

- Whines = worry, needs

Recognizing situations that give your Schnauzer concern such as reactive dogs, strangers, or loud noises lets you remove them or counter-condition with positive associations. Understanding dog body language boosts your capacity to communicate with and relate to your pooch!

Chapter Five

Teaching Basic Cues

Sit, Stay, Come, Down, Heel

Teaching your Miniature Schnauzer fundamental obedience signals through positive reinforcement gives a solid foundation for additional training. Here are tips for the core commands:

Sit

- Hold a goodie at your dog's nose level and slowly elevate it above their head until they tip back into a seat. Mark and reward.
- Repeat until they start sitting by simply your hand gesture. Then add a verbal "sit" cue.
- Practice sitting frequently before meals, walks, play, and as a default activity.

Down

- Ask for a seat first, then hold a reward in front of
their nose. Slowly lower the treat straight down to
the floor. Their heads will follow.
- Mark and reward down position. Build up to
adding a hand signal and "down" verbal cue.
- Make sure the dog is fully lying down, not simply
squatting.

Stay

- After your dog sits or downs, say "stay", take a few
steps back, and stop 5-10 seconds before returning
to reward.
- Gradually increase duration. Vary locations for
distraction. Give an added "stay" if they shatter.
- Reward for maintaining your position until you
release them. Frequent brief sessions yield
outcomes.

Come

- Say their name cheerfully, pat your legs, and run backward enticing them to chase you for a reward.
- Progress to calling from short distances using a long lead if needed at first. Always reward coming to you.
- Randomly ask to come throughout walks or play so kids don't associate it simply with a fun ending.

Heel

- With your dog on a leash in a seat, step out and encourage walking in perfect heel position (by your side looking ahead). Mark and reward correct heel position multiple steps at a time.
- Use snacks held to your waist as a lure initially. Wean off over time by rewarding intermittently.
- Require an attentive heel stance before permitting sniffing or wandering on walks.

Use brief, interesting sessions to develop these basic cues. Your Schnauzer will pick them up quickly through positive reinforcement training!

Loose Leash Walking

Teaching loose-leash walking prevents dragging and creates a delightful stroll for you both. Follow these steps:

Use Proper Equipment

- Choose a front-attack no-pull harness that closes your dog's range of motion when they pull. Head halters help inhibit pulling by blocking the lips.
- Proper fit is vital. Check size often as your pooch grows.
- Hold the leash firmly but without repetitively yanking.

Reward Your Side

- Praise and treat whenever your pooch is at your side or just behind you. Reward often for the job you want.
- Use high-value rewards initially to grab their interest. Phase out food rewards over time.
- If your pup goes ahead, stop moving and call back to your side.

Use Premack Principle

- The Premack principle uses your dog's drive to explore as a reward for staying by your side.
- Allow sniffing, roving, or play only after a time of focused heel walking.
- Then redirect back to your side. This underscores that remaining close to you grants them freedom.

Practice Turns

- Randomly change direction during the walk. Reward your pup for staying with you on turns instead of blasting ahead.
- Maintaining focus on you in any direction enhances response.

Walk with Purpose

- Stroll at a brisk, purposeful pace. This focuses your dog's energy on moving forward.
- Wandering slowly can encourage your dog to take the lead and pull.

If your Schnauzer pulls or acts excitedly, interrupt and get attention back with an "Eh eh!" sound. Resume walking only after the leash is slack again. Stay positive - they will progress with consistency.

Drop It and Leave It

Teaching "drop it" and "leave it" cues prevents your Mini Schnauzer from consuming dangerous or undesired items. Here's how to train them:

Drop It

Start with something your dog is willing to give up quickly like a low-value toy.

- Give the object and let your dog hold it briefly. Say "drop it" and offer a high-value goodie in exchange. Praise when they release the item for the treat.

- Practice trades regularly, upgrading to better toys. Eventually, they learn to give up stuff merely for your "drop it" cue without needing the treat swap each time.

- If they won't obey, gently hold their snout closed for a few seconds so the thing falls out naturally. Praise.

Leave It

Place a low-value reward on the floor and cover it with your hand as your dog approaches. Say "Leave it." Lift your hands only after they stop advancing. Praise and reward that self-control.

- Next practice with higher-value products and food drops during meals. Reward any reluctance at your "leave it" trigger.

- Increase difficulty by dropping food as you walk so they have to halt and not eat the bait.

Both these skills demand impulse control. Go in tiny stages celebrating minor successes. With time and proofing, your Mini Schnauzer will learn to defer to you when you urge them to ignore attractive items or drop prohibited ones. Valuable cues for safety!

Chapter Six

Obedience Training

Advanced Cues and Commands

Once your Miniature Schnauzer has mastered basic obedience, you can train more advanced behaviors using positive reinforcement. Here are some fun tricks and practical clues to try:

Shake - Gently lift your dog's paw and say "Shake." Repeat and reward paw lifts. Add your cue word right before they lift.

High Five - With your hand lifted, guide your dog to jump up and touch their nose to your palm. Reward touches. Add a "High five" cue.

Spin - Lure your dog in a circle with a reward to get motion started. Say "Spin" as they turn. Reward full rotations.

Crawl - Capture your dog crawling on their belly naturally or lure it with a goodie under a low chair. Say "Crawl" and praise forward belly motions.

Speak - Say "Speak" when your dog barks. Reward successive barks on command with rewards. Dogs often take this up quickly.

Quiet - When your dog barks, hold a treat in your fist and wait for any halt in barking before rewarding. The interval increases longer with practice and the command "Quiet."

Kiss - Say "Kiss" and touch your cheek when your dog kisses your face. Reward licks delivered on just the prompt.

Wave - Start by elevating your dog's paw and rewarding it. Say "Wave" right before elevating the paw. Most dogs will generalize this skill.

Roll Over - Guide your dog to roll using a luring reward. Once the motion is learned, add your vocal "Rollover" cue directly before.

These more complex behaviors increase your communication, stimulate your Mini Schnauzer mentally, and impress people with your dog's smarts! Practice new cues favorably in 5-minute sessions numerous times a day.

Off-Leash Control

Off-leash control provides your Miniature Schnauzer freedom to play and explore while keeping attentive to your commands. Follow these steps to train consistent off-leash manners:

Ensure Solid On-Leash Skills

- Start by ensuring your Mini Schnauzer has outstanding leash manners and recall. If not, concentrate on their attention with those talents first.
- Off-leash freedom is a luxury acquired through training, not a right. Wait until your dog's obedience is solid.

Start in Distraction Areas

- Begin off-leash training in enclosed, low-distraction areas like your backyard, a tennis court, or a vacant dog park.
- High stimuli locations make paying attention to you more challenging for your dog.

Reward Attention

- Bring delectable treats on walks and hikes and reward regular check-ins and eye contact with your dog. This promotes remaining attentive to you.
- Occasionally call your dog back simply to reward it with a goodie before releasing it to play again.

Use a Long Line

- Attach a 20 or 30-foot length rope to your dog's collar or harness during early off-leash excursions. This allows stopping them from running off if needed.
- But don't rely on it. Continue rewarding your dog for loose leash training to establish excellent habits.

Practice Emergency Recalls

- Set up practice scenarios when you urgently call your dog back to you from play, then reward generously with food and praise.
- This establishes arriving when called even while heavily distracted.

Take It Slowly

- Gradually allow your dog more freedom in low-distraction settings as their skills improve over numerous sessions.
- If they start rejecting commands, go back to a long line until their compliance is reliable again.

With constant positive reinforcement training, your Miniature Schnauzer will develop outstanding off-leash etiquette and recall abilities for safety and fun!

Competition Obedience Overview

Obedience competitions like rallies, obedience trials, and freestyle provide Miniature Schnauzers a chance to show off their training. Here's an overview of each event:

AKC Obedience Trials

- The classic obedience trial has the dog and handler accomplish a sequence of predefined skills:
- Healing patterns - The dog exactly matches the handler's pace and position
- Stays - Sit and down with the handler at a distance
- Recall - dog swiftly comes on order
- Retrieve - dog fetches things and presents them to the hand
- Scent work - locating scent articles
- Additional moves - jumping, drop on recall, directed retrieve

- Judging based on precision, temperament, and coordination between dog and handler.

- Titling levels: Companion Dog (CD), Companion Dog Excellent (CDX), Utility Dog (UD), Utility Dog Excellent (UDX)

AKC Rally Trials

- Performed at a brisk pace with the dog off-leash. Handler observes numbered signs instructing maneuvers:
- Starts, turns, spins, side-steps
- Stays, downs, recalls
- Jumps, tunnels, weave poles

- Focus on enthusiasm and accuracy. Less rigorous than obedience.

- Titling levels: Rally Novice (RN), Rally Advanced (RA), Rally Excellent (RE)

Competitive Canine Freestyle

- Flashy choreographed routine set to music displaying obedience skills
- Creative healing patterns, stunts, spins, leg weaving, and more
- Costumes and props allowed

- Judged on choreography complexity, precision, excitement

While not compulsory, competing is an exciting aim for dogs and handlers. It enhances training skills and the bond between you and your Miniature Schnauzer. Choose the venue that best fits your dog's strengths and your interests!

Chapter Seven

Potty Training

Creating a Routine

Establishing a consistent toilet schedule is crucial to properly housetraining your Miniature Schnauzer puppy. Follow these tips:

Take Out Frequently

- Take your puppy outdoors to potty every 30 minutes to an hour when they're active and playing.
- Puppies physically can't regulate their bladders for long when young. Frequent bathroom breaks prevent accidents.

Go Out After Meals

- Your puppy will likely need to relieve themselves 5-15 minutes after eating. Escort them outside immediately following meal sessions.

Visit Potty Spot First Thing

- As soon as your puppy departs their crate or sleeping space in the morning, rush them right outdoors to their toilet spot. Praise and praise toilets.

Go Out Before Bedtime

- Right before you go to sleep for the night, take your puppy out one last time. This helps minimize accidents overnight.

Watch for Signals

- When your dog suddenly starts circling, sniffing, or sitting inside, swiftly scoop them up and dash outside. Reward them for finishing their business at the right spot.

Supervise Closely

- When indoors, keep your puppy in view at all times. This allows you to identify toilet cues and swiftly divert them outside. Confine them if needed.

Stay Patient

- Puppies don't have full bladder control until 6 months of age. Accidents will happen along the road. Stick to your routine consistently and they'll get there.

Creating a predictable, frequent potty routine and rewarding triumphs builds excellent restroom habits. Your dog will rapidly understand that outside is the place to go.

Crate Training

Crate training harnesses your Miniature Schnauzer's natural den instincts to help with toilet training and safety. Follow these tips:

Choose Appropriate Crate

Select a properly sized crate - just big enough for your dog to stand, turn around, and lie down. Too much space allows removal. Use a dividing panel to alter the size as your puppy develops.

Make It Inviting

Line the crate with blankets and familiar scents like their favorite toy. Place in a social area like the living room. Cover the top and sides to feel more den-like if your dog appears uncomfortable at first.

Use for Naps and Bedtime

Encourage your Mini Schnauzer to routinely nap and sleep in their crate during the day and night. This prevents nighttime unrest and establishes it as a bedroom.

Reward Entering

Toss goodies and toys inside so your puppy enters voluntarily. Praise and reward any step toward entering. Feed your dog in the open crate to develop pleasant associations.

Keep Sessions Short At First

When first introducing the crate, keep sessions brief - just 10-20 minutes - to reduce complaining and restlessness. Reward quiet crate behavior. Gradually lengthen the crating duration.

Take Directly Outside

As soon as you open the crate door, immediately guide your puppy outside to their toilet area. They won't want to pollute their den, therefore potties are likely!

Avoid Using it as Punishment

Never use the kennel for punishment or force your hesitant dog inside. This weakens the crate as a joyful retreat. Always make it a voluntary, good space.

With time and rewards, your Mini Schnauzer will come to consider their kennel as their particular den. This makes housetraining easy and gives your pup a secure space of their own.

Dealing with Accidents

No matter how attentive, toilet training mistakes often happen with puppies and older dogs. Here is how to correctly respond to accidents:

Stay Calm

When you catch your Mini Schnauzer in the act of eliminating inside, calmly interrupt with an "Oops!" or "Outside!" Avoid screaming or scaring them, which might hamper housetraining.

Immediately Redirect Outside

Pick up your dog mid-accident if possible and take them directly to their right potty spot. Finish going outside, then provide plenty of praise and treats when they do.

Clean Thoroughly

Use an enzymatic rather than detergent-based cleanser to break down urine and stool deposits. Avoid ammonia cleaners, which smell like urine to dogs. Blot, don't rub, urine to avoid spreading scent messages.

Prevent Access

If certain rooms or surfaces provide frequent problems, use baby gates, exercise pens, and locked doors to block access until potty training develops. Tether your dog to you if needed.

Analyze Cause

Consider whether an underlying medical issue like UTI or gastrointestinal trouble is contributing to accidents. Also watch for breaches in monitoring, access to previously dirty places, or schedule changes.

Reinforce Training

Respond by reinforcing potty training from square one again. Increase oversight and independence only with regular success. Consider going back to limiting access if troubles continue.

Remain Positive

Never scold or chastise your dog after the fact for accidents. They don't comprehend. Stay optimistic during the retraining process. Consistency and rewards lead to success.

Potty training road bumps are typical. Stick to a routine, restrict access if needed, completely clean messes, and redirect firmly. Your Mini Schnauzer will get back on track!

Chapter Eight

Stopping Unwanted Behaviors

Barking, Begging, Jumping Up

Miniature Schnauzers are prone to several unwanted behaviors like barking, begging, and jumping up. Here are positive approaches to minimize these habits:

Barking

- Determine the cause - wants, boredom, fear, separation anxiety. Address the root motivation.
- Teach a "Quiet" cue using goodies to reward pauses in barking and develop duration.
- Redirect to calm actions incompatible with barking like sit or down stays.

- Use background white noise to mask triggers. Exercise before high stimulus times.
- For barking, ignore the behavior and praise silence before giving your dog what they want.

Begging

- Don't give in to begging – this fosters pushy conduct.
- Teach an alternate behavior like "go to your mat" using incentives. Enforce during meals.
- Feed your dog before you sit down to eat so they're not as hungry.
- Keep people's foods out of reach and train a solid "leave it."
- Have guests sprinkle treats on the floor when entering to avoid jumping up for food.

Jumping Up

- Turn aside and fold your arms anytime your dog jumps, ignoring them until all four paws are on the floor. Then softly pat and reward the relaxed conduct.

- Ask for a seat immediately upon people arriving which physically prohibits jumping.
- Discourage jumping before it starts by educating your dog to go to their mat when people enter.
- Avoid touching your dog without all four paws down or giving attention if they jump.

Stay positive - screaming or punishing these behaviors typically backfires. Redirecting to desirable actions and praising those is most successful.

Digging, Chewing Destruction

Digging or destructive chewing activities in Miniature Schnauzers frequently result from boredom, stress, or lack of activity. Here are the solutions:

Digging

- Provide an acceptable digging trench with buried toys to satisfy impulses. Teach a "go dig" cue guiding your dog there.
- Bury treats around the yard randomly so they dig expecting a reward. Teach them to dig only on cue.
- Interrupt unwanted digging and redirect to a toy. Limit access if needed until the habit fades.
- Ensure your dog receives appropriate exercise and mental stimulation daily.

Chewing Destruction

- Puppy-proof houses by removing or preventing access to attractive objects. Keep shoes, remotes, and books out of reach.
- Provide a wide assortment of chew toys and rotate them periodically to keep them interesting.
- Coat appealing improper goods with bitter anti-chew spray.

- Teach a good "leave it" signal and divert gnawing to sanctioned toys.
- Identify factors that may be triggering destructive behavior and lessen or eliminate them.
- Increase regular exercise, training sessions, and puzzle toys. A fatigued dog is less apt to chew.
- Crate your dog when you're away and can't supervise until the habit resolves.

Ripping Up Objects

- Remove access to paper things including toilet paper, mail, books, and cardboard.
- Teach a "drop it" cue to release prohibited goods. Exchange for a treat.
- Redirect playfulness to pull toys and other rough chews.
- Having delectable chews available provides an acceptable outlet for play-biting behavior.

Patience and addressing the main cause of undesired chewing or digging is crucial. Manage the environment, watch constantly, and reward approved outlets for natural behaviors.

Aggression and Nipping

Aggressive reactions in Miniature Schnauzers like snarling, snapping, or biting necessitate prompt intervention. Here are tips:

Identify Trigger

Carefully assess what particularly provokes the aggressive response - food, toys, handling, strangers, other dogs? Knowing the context helps establish solutions.

Interrupt Behavior

At the first hint of violence like raised hackles, stiffening, or growling, rapidly disrupt by surprising with a loud "Eh eh!" or clap. Redirect their attention to a sit or concentration cue.

Consult a Trainer

For significant aggressiveness, promptly consult a credentialed trainer or behaviorist. They can provide specific behavior modification regimens geared to your dog. This is not a DIY situation.

Counter Condition Triggers

Systematically concentrate on linking the aggression triggers with happy experiences like food treats instead of frightened ones. Very gradually affect their emotional response.

Avoid Punishment

Punishing violent actions typically worsens them. Harsh corrections can make dogs scared and provoke greater aggressiveness. Always employ reward-based modification.

Consider Medications

In extreme circumstances, medicines may assist take the edge off while undertaking behavior modification therapy. Talk to your veterinarian. Usually, this is accompanied by training.

Nipping and Mouthing

For play nipping and biting during puppyhood or excitement:

- Carry chew toys to redirect biting onto acceptable objects

- Say "Enough!" firmly and withdraw all attention when biting gets too hard

- Allow contact only when the mouth is quiet and gentle

- Avoid wrestling or aggressive play that encourages biting

The key is discovering the underlying motivation for aggression and altering that emotional response through positive training. Never ignore or delay addressing aggressive conduct – it just gets worse.

Chapter Nine

Advanced Training Skills

Agility Training

Agility is a fun, fast-paced canine sport that Miniature Schnauzers often excel in. Here's an introduction to getting started with agility:

Find a Class or Club

Look for group agility sessions at nearby training facilities, parks, or clubs. Beginner sessions focus on foundation skills without impediments. Classes provide structure and instruction.

Train Basic Obedience First

Start with a good foundation in fundamental obedience. Skills like a reliable "sit," "down," "stay," and arriving when called are vital for navigating courses off-leash.

Socialize to Equipment

Gradually expose your Mini Schnauzer to all the agility obstacles before attempting full courses. Let them explore and earn goodies on stationary equipment first. Build confidence.

Introduce One Obstacle at a Time

Systematically train each obstacle independently using shaping and rewards before merging several together. Mastering elements in isolation first puts you both up for success.

Go at Your Dog's Pace

Let your Mini Schnauzer choose the speed and challenge level. Avoid shoving them through obstructions. Always make training experiences positive by working inside your dog's comfort zone.

Use Targets and Lures

Hold objects like treats or toys beyond obstacles to encourage your dog via the appropriate path. Fade lures over time by rewarding intermittently.

Practice Handling Skills

Handlers direct the dog through courses using body movement and vocal signals. Practice using subtle hints and navigating courses without your dog first. Clear communication is crucial.

Make It Fun!

Always provide praise and awards enthusiastically. End sessions on a high note leaving your dog wanting more. Avoid drill-like repetition. Mix up obstacle orders to retain interest.

Agility strengthens the link between you and your Mini Schnauzer. Look for a lesson dedicated to beginners to get started on the appropriate fundamentals. Your dog will thrill to the fun trials!

Scent Detection

Scent detection leverages Miniature Schnauzers' strong noses and hunts drive. Fun nose work games and sports include:

Scent Detection Games

- Hide and Seek – Hide little snacks throughout the house and shout "Find it!" as your dog searches by scent.

- Which Hand? - Put a treat in one closed hand. Let your dog sniff and paw at the correct hand.

- Find the Toy - Have your dog sit while you hide a beloved toy in plain sight. Send them to search using "Find your [toy name]!"

- Trail Games - Drag toys scented with treats around the yard in patterns for your dog to follow.

These games promote confidence in using their nose and get them acclimated to looking for certain scents.

AKC Scent Work

This sport involves dogs identifying target scents hidden in containers or settings and alerting their handlers. Classes and trials include:

- Container hunt - Birch, anise, clove fragrances hidden in boxes

- Interior search - Finding perfumed cotton swabs in rooms

- Exterior search - Seeking fragrant objects strewn outside

- Buried search - Locating fragrant objects underground

Scent work promotes cerebral stimulation and satisfies sniffing inclinations. Mini Schnauzers love the challenge!

K9 Nose Work

Developed from detection dog principles, K9 Nose Work teaches dogs to discover real-world target odors. Classes involve:

- Birch oil - Start with this new aroma before adding food/toy odors

- Food aroma - Seeking hot dogs, cheese, etc.

- Toy smell - Finding scented toys

- Environmental fragrance - Alerting on odors already present in the search area

Dogs acquire final response behaviors like sitting, down, or barking to alert the location. Trials offer titles.

NACSW Nosework

The National Association of Canine Scent Work offers classes and trials in:

- Container search
- Interior search
- Exterior search
- Buried search
- Detection of birch, anise, clove scents

This program focuses on precision, difficulty, and scents mimicking genuine working detecting canines.

Scent work is an engaging activity for Mini Schnauzers' acute noses. Fun games can practice abilities for competition if needed.

Tricks and Games

Teaching your Miniature Schnauzer interesting skills keeps their mind occupied and deepens your bond. Here are more fun tricks to try:

Play Dead

- Say "Bang!" then gently roll your dog onto their side. Praise and reward the position.

- Repeat until they start going down on simply your vocal command. Then write "Play dead!"

Pray

- Shape front paws raising into begging positions with rewards.

- Add the verbal cue "Pray!" when in position. Can form hind legs kneeling too.

Roll Over

- Lure the dog's nose down to the ground and guide the body in a sideways roll. Reward during the roll.

- Fade lure and add a "Roll over!" vocal signal as they master the motion.

Crawl

- Capture or encourage forward belly movement with rewards down to the ground.

- Say "Crawl" each time they move forward on their belly. Reward progress.

Leg Weaves

- With your dog facing you, step forward between their legs, tempting them with a goodie. Reward as they shift back legs.

- Gradually incorporate weaving forward and backward between your legs on command.

Catch Food Tossed in Air

- Toss little goodies gently underhand to be grabbed. Reward successful catches.

- Increase height and challenge as coordination develops.

Costume Fun

- Help your dog try on goofy outfits like hats, sunglasses, and capes. Capture their genuine reactions and interactions. Share the exciting photographs and videos!

Incorporating new techniques into training sessions increases abilities, stimulates your Mini Schnauzer psychologically, and strengthens your fun bond together!

Chapter Ten

Grooming Your Miniature Schnauzer

Coat Care and Stripping

The Miniature Schnauzer's unusual wiry coat requires frequent grooming and stripping to retain its texture and appearance. Here are tips:

Daily Brushing

- Brush the coat thoroughly each day to eliminate debris, distribute oils, and prevent matting.
- Use a firm bristle brush to work down to the skin over all regions.
- Go section by section against the coat growth trend.

- Pay additional care to bulkier parts like the legs, belly, and pants.

Bathing

- Bathe every 3-6 weeks or when the coat becomes soiled with a dog-specific shampoo.
- Avoid over-bathing, which can dry out their skin and coat.
- Dry thoroughly and brush out after to fluff and straighten the coat.

Monthly Stripping

- Coat stripping by hand or with a stripping knife scrapes off dead hairs to stimulate new growth.
- Focus on the furnishings, pants, and beard which grow scruffy looking when hair fades.
- Go segment by section carefully plucking dead hairs in the direction they grow.
- Remove the undercoat in thicker places with a shedding blade.

Yearly Clipping

- Most pet Schnauzers need a clipper to shave down once or twice a year to reset the coat instead of full hand stripping.
- Leave 1-2 inches of length utilizing proper blade guards.
- Start anew with new coat growth. Hand strip and trim furniture.

Ear Cleaning

- Pluck extra hair from ear canals monthly with tweezers to facilitate airflow.
- Clean inside ears with a veterinarian-recommended solution and cotton balls.
- Never introduce things into ear canals.

Nail Trimming

- Trim nails periodically to prevent splits and overgrowth. Use dog nail clippers and file any rough edges.
- Introduce handling paws early to adapt them to trimming.
- Reward them with sweets during trims to develop pleasant associations.

Regular grooming keeps your Mini Schnauzer looking dapper while boosting skin and coat health. Proper practices avoid matting and keep their unique rugged appearance.

Nail Trimming

Trimming your Miniature Schnauzer's nails regularly minimizes splits and overgrowth. Follow these recommendations for safer, stress-free trims:

Introduce Handling Early

- As a puppy, softly touch paws frequently, rewarding calm responses.
- Briefly hold paws and press on nails to get them acquainted with the sensation.
- Make paw handling a frequent, positive experience.

Use Proper Equipment

- Invest in quality guillotine-style dog nail clippers suited for your dog's size. Avoid human trimmers.
- Only cut a small bit at a time. Have a styptic powder on hand.
- Use a fine file/grinder to smooth sharp edges.

Position Properly

- Have your dog sit, lie down, or stand with their rear against your stomach for support.
- Hold a front paw beneath your arm to expand it. Reward them in this position.

- Or position them on an elevated platform at waist height for easy access.

Work Methodically

- Extend one paw at a time fully to show the nails. Reward.
- Snip just the clear area of a few nails at one visit. Don't rush.
- Give a treat after each nail to generate pleasant thoughts about the process.

Watch the Quick

- Avoid severing the blood supply (quick) inside nails by merely partially trimming tips.
- If bleeding occurs, apply styptic powder to halt it.

Make Regular Trims Part of Routine

- Add trims to your usual grooming practice like weekly brushing to normalize them.

- Target moments when your dog is already quiet and relaxed, like after exercise.

Keep each session low stress, quitting at any sign of difficulty. Regular, gradual exposure to handling, sounds, and feelings will lead to a pet who tolerates nail care. Be patient - it's a training process.

Cleaning Wrinkles and Folds

Dogs like Miniature Schnauzers with facial wrinkles, lip folds, and droopy ears need them cleaned regularly to prevent infections. Here's how:

Face and Neck Wrinkles

- Wipe deep facial folds daily with a moist washcloth to remove dirt and debris.
- Dry completely. Apply antifungal powder to prevent yeast infections.

- Check for reddish skin, irritation, or odor indicating infection. Seek medicine if needed.

Lip Folds

- Pull apart lip folds to access nooks and wipe clean with a gentle moist cloth.
- Swab beneath lips, chin, and beard. Dry thoroughly.
- Monitor moisture and debris buildup that might cause dermatitis.

Ears

- Gently remove excess wax and dirt from outer ears and canal openings with a cleaning solution on cotton balls.
- Pluck extra hair from canals weekly with tweezers.
- Check for redness, discharge, or head shaking indicating infection.

Tail Pocket

- Lift the tail and clean the underside with a damp towel if the region feels moist or dusty.
- Dry completely. Apply antibiotic ointment if red or inflamed.
- Ensure anal glands are not compromised. See a vet for an expression if needed.

Paws

- Wipe between paw pads after outdoor activities to remove debris.
- Apply balm if pads look dry or cracked.

Nose

- Use a warm, wet towel to gently wipe nasal crevices. Avoid excessive moisture inside nostrils.
- Dry completely. Apply pet-safe snood balm if needed.

Regular cleaning reduces germs and yeast overgrowth that can form in moist skin creases. Make it part of your grooming practice and look for any worrying indicators of infection. Keeping wrinkles clean promotes health and comfort.

Chapter Eleven

Keeping Your Miniature Schnauzer Healthy

Nutrition and Exercise Needs

Proper nutrition and exercise are crucial to your Miniature Schnauzer's health. Here are some tips:

Nutrition

- Feed a high-quality commercial or home-cooked feed formulated for your dog's age and activity level.

- Provide measured meals rather than free feeding to prevent obesity.

- Choose a meal specific to Schnauzers if feasible that accounts for predispositions such as hyperlipidemia.

- Supplement with oils or joint supplements as needed for skin/coat or mobility difficulties.

- Provide fresh water at all times - refresh and wash dishes periodically.

- Avoid people's food, which can lead to pancreatitis and other complications.

Exercise Needs

- Miniature Schnauzers need 30-60 minutes of exercise every day.

- Brisk walks, jogging, trekking, swimming, and fetch are terrific hobbies.

- Mental exercise through training sessions and puzzle toys also helps fatigue them.

- Ensure they have both physical and mental stimulation. A bored Schnauzer can be destructive.

- Play games like hide and seek using their natural rat-hunting instincts.

- Schnauzers can be energetic pullers and joggers if properly conditioned.

Preventing Obesity

- Measure food carefully and limit snacks. Avoid free-feeding.

- Encourage activity daily through walks, play, and training.

- Use food puzzle toys to make mealtime an activity.

- Monitor weight periodically and alter meals if needed. Consult your vet.

- Swap goodies for praise/pets when possible. Choose low-calorie alternatives.

Providing the correct nutrition and exercise regimen enhances your Schnauzer's lifelong health, mobility, energy levels, and ideal weight. Work with your vet to develop a plan for your dog's needs.

Veterinary Care and Prevention

Establishing preventive veterinary care helps your Miniature Schnauzer live a long, healthy life. Here are tips:

Annual Exams

- Schedule annual wellness checks to completely assess health.
- Bloodwork, urinalysis, dental exams, and parasite screening are important.
- Discuss any concerns and keep your dog's vaccines up to date.

Dental Care

- Miniature Schnauzers are prone to dental problems so plan frequent cleanings.
- Brush teeth and provide chews to preserve health between cleanings.
- Have your vet investigate any signs of dental pain, loose teeth, or foul breath.

Preventatives

- Use monthly heartworm, flea, and tick prevention medicine year round or as suggested in your area.
- Schnauzers are extremely susceptible to these harmful parasites. Prevention is key.

Immunizations

- Puppies need a series of essential immunizations on a predetermined schedule - your vet advises you on timing.
- Adults need boosters for distemper, adenovirus, and parvovirus every 3 years.
- Leptospirosis, Lyme, influenza, and kennel cough immunizations may also be suggested.

Genetic Testing

- Reputable breeders examine for concerns including hyperlipidemia, eye disease, and liver illness.
- Further testing can measure risks for von Willebrand's illness, thyroid issues, and Deafness.
- Results allow breeding efforts to lower the likelihood of these genetic disorders.

Prompt Intervention

- Because Schnauzers hide illness well, observe for slight changes in energy, appetite, or behavior that could suggest a problem.
- Don't delay in getting veterinarian assessments for any problems. Proactive care is crucial.

Working closely with your vet provides the finest preventative treatment and early identification of any health issues. Being watchful and proactive provides your Mini Schnauzer their greatest shot for a long, comfortable life.

Monitoring Behavior and Happiness

In-tune owners learn to read their Miniature Schnauzer's signs. Monitor these well-being indicators:

Energy Level

- Take note if your ordinarily lively Schnauzer slows down, tires quickly, or appears lethargic. This often signifies disease or suffering.

Appetite Changes

- Appetite loss can signify dental disease, gastrointestinal disorders, or other systemic ailments.

- Sudden increased hunger may suggest diabetes or hyperadrenocorticism.

Elimination Habits

- Any toilet accidents after training, new straining or discomfort, changes in frequency or amount of urine/stool, or altered consistency need a veterinary inspection.

Weight Loss/Gain

- Visible weight loss or gain if not consciously intended through diet modification requires additional diagnostics - visit your vet.

Coat and Skin Condition

- Note any changes in coat texture or symptoms of skin discomfort such as chewing, rubbing, or scooting. Skin concerns are common in Schnauzers.

Mood Changes

- Take note if your gregarious dog becomes reclusive or irritated, which can indicate discomfort or disease.

Activity Preferences

- Observe any shifts in your dog's preferred activities. Aversion to items they previously enjoyed may suggest physical or emotional suffering.

Body Sensitivity

- Does your dog shrink away, whimper, or snap when handled in a certain spot? This can suggest injury or orthopedic pain. Have your vet evaluate.

Catching minor adjustments early helps pinpoint abnormalities before they become severe. Monitoring well-being markers should be part of your daily caretaking regimen. Know what's usual for your unique Schnauzer.

20 homemade food recipe ideas for a Miniature Schnauzer with ingredients and preparation instructions

1. Homemade Turkey and Sweet Potato Dog Bites:

- Ingredients:
- 1 cup ground turkey
- 1/2 cup cooked and mashed sweet potato
- 1/4 cup oat flour - 1 egg

- Instructions:
  1. Preheat the oven to 350°F (175°C).
  2. In a bowl, mix ground turkey, mashed sweet potato, oat flour, and beaten egg until well blended.

3. Roll the mixture into small balls and lay them on a baking sheet.

4. Bake for 15-20 minutes until golden brown and cooked thoroughly.

2. Chicken and Carrot Dog Muffins:

- Ingredients:
- 1 cup shredded chicken
- 1/2 cup grated carrot
- 1/4 cup whole wheat flour
- 1 egg

- Instructions:
1. Preheat the oven to 350°F (175°C).

2. Mix shredded chicken, grated carrot, whole wheat flour, and beaten egg in a bowl.

3. Spoon the mixture into a prepared small muffin tray.

4. Bake for 12-15 minutes until the muffins are firm and brown.

3. Peanut Butter and Banana Pupcakes:

- Ingredients:
- 1 ripe banana, mashed
- 1/4 cup peanut butter
- 1/2 cup whole wheat flour
- 1/2 teaspoon baking soda

- Instructions:
   1. Preheat the oven to 350°F (175°C).
   2. In a bowl, add mashed banana, peanut butter, whole wheat flour, and baking soda.
   3. Spoon the batter into cupcake liners in a tiny cupcake tray.
   4. Bake for 10-12 minutes until a toothpick comes out clean.

4. Salmon and Sweet Potato Dog Cookies:

- Ingredients:
- 1/2 cup canned salmon, drained and flaked
- 1/2 cup cooked and mashed sweet potato

- 1 cup oat flour

- 1 egg

  - Instructions:

    1. Preheat the oven to 325°F (163°C).

    2. Mix salmon, mashed sweet potato, oat flour, and beaten egg in a bowl.

    3. Roll out the dough and use cookie cutters to create shapes.

    4. Bake for 15-20 minutes until the rims are golden brown.

5. Beef and Spinach Doggy Meatballs:

  - Ingredients:
- 1/2 cup minced beef
- 1/2 cup finely chopped spinach
- 1/4 cup grated Parmesan cheese
- 1/4 cup breadcrumbs
- 1 egg

  - Instructions:

1. Preheat the oven to 375°F (190°C).

2. Combine ground beef, chopped spinach, Parmesan cheese, breadcrumbs, and beaten egg in a bowl.

3. Shape the mixture into tiny meatballs and lay them on a baking sheet.

4. Bake for 20-25 minutes until the meatballs are cooked through and browned.

6. Cheesy Zucchini and Chicken Biscuits:

- Ingredients:
- 1/2 cup shredded cooked chicken
- 1/2 cup shredded zucchini, drained
- 1/4 cup grated cheddar cheese
- 1/4 cup coconut flour
- 1 egg

- Instructions:

1. Preheat the oven to 350°F (175°C).

2. Mix shredded chicken, shredded zucchini, cheddar cheese, coconut flour, and beaten egg in a bowl.

3. Form little biscuit shapes and set them on a baking pan.

4. Bake for 15-18 minutes until the biscuits are firm and slightly golden.

7. Quinoa and Turkey Stew for Pups:

- Ingredients:
- 1/2 cup cooked quinoa
- 1/2 cup ground turkey
- 1/4 cup finely chopped green beans
- 1/4 cup diced pumpkin
- 1 cup low-sodium chicken broth

- Instructions:

1. In a pot, combine cooked quinoa, ground turkey, green beans, pumpkin, and chicken broth.

2. Cook over medium heat until the turkey is fully cooked and the vegetables are soft.

3. Let it cool before serving it to your Miniature Schnauzer.

8. Blueberry and Oat Doggy Pancakes:

- Ingredients:
- 1/2 cup blueberries (fresh or frozen)
- 1/2 cup rolled oats
- 1/4 cup plain yogurt
- 1 egg

- Instructions:

1. Blend blueberries, rolled oats, plain yogurt, and beaten egg in a food processor.

2. Pour small amounts of batter onto a hot, greased griddle to form micro pancakes.

3. Cook until bubbles appear on the surface, then flip and cook the other side.

9. Carrot and Apple Dog Treats:

- Ingredients:

- 1 cup shredded carrot

- 1 cup grated apple

- 1/2 cup oat flour

- 1/4 cup coconut oil, melted

- Instructions:

1. Preheat the oven to 350°F (175°C).

2. Mix grated carrot, grated apple, oat flour, and melted coconut oil in a bowl.

3. Drop spoonfuls of the mixture onto a baking sheet.

4. Bake for 12-15 minutes until the cookies are golden brown.

10. Salmon and Potato Popsicles:

- Ingredients:

- 1/2 cup canned salmon, mashed

- 1/2 cup mashed sweet potato

- 1 cup low-sodium chicken broth

- Instructions:

1. In a bowl, combine mashed salmon, mashed sweet potato, and chicken broth.

2. Pour the mixture into small molds or ice cube pans.

3. Freeze until solid, then pop out and serve as a refreshing treat.

11. Pumpkin and Turkey Doggy Muffins:

- Ingredients:
- 1/2 cup canned pumpkin puree
- 1/2 cup ground turkey
- 1/4 cup almond flour
- 1/4 cup shredded carrot
- 1 egg

- Instructions:
1. Preheat the oven to 350°F (175°C).

2. Mix pumpkin puree, ground turkey, almond flour, shredded carrot, and beaten egg in a bowl.

3. Spoon the batter into a mini muffin tray.

4. Bake for 15-18 minutes until the muffins are cooked through.

12. Spinach and Chicken Doggy Omelette:

- Ingredients:
- 1/2 cup cooked and shredded chicken
- 1/2 cup chopped fresh spinach
- 1 egg

- Instructions:
   1. In a bowl, whisk the egg and add in shredded chicken and chopped spinach.
   2. Pour the mixture into an oiled skillet and heat until the egg is set.
   3. Allow it to cool before cutting it into bite-sized pieces.

13. Sweet Potato and Peanut Butter Popsicles:

- Ingredients:

- 1/2 cup mashed sweet potato

- 2 teaspoons peanut butter

- 1 cup plain yogurt

- Instructions:

1. Mix mashed sweet potato, peanut butter, and yogurt in a bowl.

2. Pour the mixture into molds or ice cube trays.

3. Freeze until solid for a lovely frozen treat.

14. Beef and Pumpkin Dog Biscuits:

- Ingredients:

- 1/2 cup lean ground beef, cooked and finely crumbled

- 1/2 cup canned pumpkin puree

- 1 cup whole wheat flour

- 1 egg

- Instructions:

1. Preheat the oven to 350°F (175°C).

2. Combine ground beef, pumpkin puree, whole wheat flour, and beaten egg.

3. Roll out the dough and cut into biscuit shapes.

4. Bake for 15-20 minutes until biscuits are golden brown.

15. Chicken and Broccoli Dog Casserole:

- Ingredients:
- 1/2 cup cooked and shredded chicken
- 1/2 cup finely chopped broccoli
- 1/4 cup brown rice, cooked
- 1/4 cup low-sodium chicken broth

- Instructions:

1. Mix shredded chicken, chopped broccoli, cooked brown rice, and chicken broth in a baking dish.

2. Bake at 350°F (175°C) for 20-25 minutes until the dish is heated thoroughly. Cool before serving.

16. Apple and Cinnamon Dog Donuts:

- Ingredients:

- 1/2 cup grated apple

- 1/2 cup oat flour

- 1/4 cup unsweetened applesauce

- 1/4 teaspoon cinnamon

 - 1 egg

- Instructions:

1. Preheat the oven to 350°F (175°C).

2. Mix grated apple, oat flour, applesauce, cinnamon, and beaten egg in a bowl.

3. Spoon the batter into a prepared mini donut pan.

4. Bake for 12-15 minutes until the donuts are firm and brown.

17. Blueberry and Chicken Pup Pizza:

- Ingredients:

- 1/2 cup cooked and shredded chicken

- 1/4 cup blueberries, mashed

- 1/4 cup mozzarella cheese, shredded
- Whole wheat tortilla

- Instructions:

1. Preheat the oven to 375°F (190°C).

2. Mix shredded chicken and mashed blueberries.

3. Spread the mixture on a whole wheat tortilla, and top with shredded mozzarella.

4. Bake for 10-12 minutes until the cheese is melted.

18. Carrot and Turkey Doggy Stir Fry:

- Ingredients:
- 1/2 cup ground turkey
- 1/2 cup finely chopped carrots
- 1/4 cup cooked brown rice
- 1 tablespoon olive oil

- Instructions:

1. In a pan, heat olive oil, add ground turkey, and cook until browned.

2. Add chopped carrots and cooked brown rice, and stir until the vegetables are soft.

3. Cool before serving.

19. Banana and Peanut Butter Frozen Pupsicles:

- Ingredients:
- 1 ripe banana, mashed
- 2 tbsp peanut butter
- 1 cup plain yogurt

- Instructions:

1. Mix mashed banana, peanut butter, and yogurt in a bowl.

2. Pour the mixture into molds or ice cube trays.

3. Freeze until solid for a delightful frozen treat.

20. Turkey and Cranberry Doggy Wraps:
- Ingredients:

- 1/2 cup cooked and shredded turkey

- 1/4 cup cranberry sauce (unsweetened)

- Whole wheat tortilla

- Instructions:

1. Spread cranberry sauce on a whole wheat tortilla.

2. Add shredded turkey and roll it into a wrap.

3. Cut into bite-sized pieces for a tasty, portable treat.